So You Got A Destiny Cards Book? *Now What?*

A GUIDE

by Paula Krueger, M.A.

INDEX

Dedicated to
The Seeker Within

"There is Something in each of us
Which impels us toward the Light."

This Little Guidebook Will Help You to:

* GIVE AN IN-DEPTH READING USING ROBERT
CAMP'S *Cards of Your Destiny Book**

* UNDERSTAND YOUR CHALLENGES *

* USE YOUR INTUITION *

ABOUT ME

In Brief

I grew up in the Midwest as a nice Christian girl. I eventually discovered the larger world of Spirituality from Buddhism to Metaphysics. I discovered the Destiny Card system over 20 years ago when my children were very small. I studied people to understand the system, and after 16 years of study began getting esoteric insight about the cards, from 'the other side.' I finally started doing professional readings.

Over the years of doing many, many readings, I have developed my own understanding of what each card means through observation, meditation, and intuition. I use the cards to predict events, but I have made emotional growth my priority.

My M.A. in Transpersonal Psychology from Naropa deepened my self-compassion and added to my skills as a counselor. FYI, I am the 7D, who have more than their fair share of developmental difficulty: the battle for self-worth through financial and relationship challenges.

My psychic ability has grown steadily through giving readings wherein the cards reveal their meanings to me. You can allow the cards to speak to you as well.

All divinatory tools are, after all, just a shared language with the Universe.

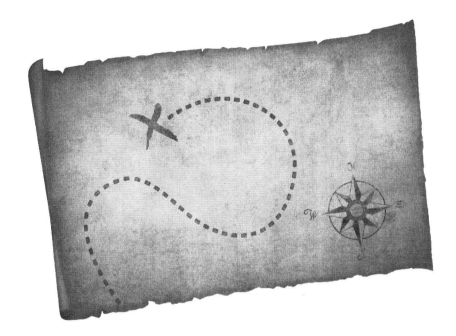

INTRODUCTION

Patience

It is so important to stay in the present, for that is where all the information you need exists. Most importantly, feel your heart. What is going on with you right now? Take a breath and answer that before proceeding.

Let's begin by focusing on your 2 cards of influence for this 52 day period. I heartily recommend NOT spending much time looking more than a couple weeks into the future.

I will show you how to turn those 2 cards into 20 or more, each of which is aimed at a specific area of your life. Your life will help you understand what the cards mean, and vice versa. Each person has a frequency for each card. The way it shows up for you may be slightly unique to you.

The main reason I am writing this book is to show you how to unlock the present with the cards, and how to unlock the cards with the present.

Treat the two 52 day cards as the meditation of the month.

Return to it every few days for reflection. Ask how your life is showing you the meaning of these cards.

These will be my abbreviations:
H=Hearts
C-Clubs
D-Diamonds
S=Spades
K=King
Q=Queen
J=Jack
COD=*Cards of Your Destiny Book* by Robert Lee Camp
C-7=Circle of 7

These 7 cards are in a group who feel intensely connected to each other: KS, JH, 9H, 8C, 7D, 2H, AC. When one shows up in your spread, the rest are implied.

THE LENSES OF TIME

The Wide Angle

Since there are 52 cards, there is a 52 year cycle. There is also a 45 and a 13 year cycle, but for our purposes here, we will start with the 7 year cycle and keep dialing down.

The 7 year cycle is felt poignantly. I don't know why we do this, but when we have an easy year we expect the next to be easy as well. Knowing what to expect, or why one year is particularly difficult will help enormously, as well as knowing how long a difficult period is likely to last.

Multiples of 7

Every age that is a multiple of 7 is your first year of that cycle. So ages 0,7,14,21,28,35,42, etc are the first year of a 7 year cycle. Each of the 7 years is ruled by a planet, always in this order: Mercury, Venus, Mars, Jupiter, Saturn, Uranus, Neptune. For example, each of the years listed above is ruled by Mercury, since each is the first year in that 7 year cycle. Let's use the cycle beginning with 35 as an example:

35: Mercury = A year for thinking, planning, learning.
36: Venus = Themes of home, women, and relationship.
37: Mars = Time for action, to get practical, deal with men.

38: Jupiter = The enterprise expands; success, blessing.
39: Saturn = Now the coach steps in. Look at obstacles.
40: Uranus = Lower intensity, put learning to use.
41: Neptune = Integration of past 7 years, envision next 7.

And then it all starts over again. This can give you some understanding about how you are feeling. People tend to be really exhausted in their Neptune year. You've been working the same "program" or "syllabus" for 7 years!!! And the Neptune year is not likely one of external productivity. You need to do the deeper work of integrating, on a somewhat unconscious level, all you have been through. And then you will begin to imagine your way into the future.

The 52 Day Cycle
In the back of your Destiny Cards book, there is a page for each month. Find your birthday, and you will see the breakdown of your 52 day cycles. (COD, p. 339)

Now go back to the two page layout for your card. The 52 day period you are in has two cards of influence. Only two cards for over 7 weeks? Yes, it's rather general. This is how you can unlock a whole file drawer of information!!!

We are going to use my cards for an example. My birthday is Aug 6. I am 50. So let's go to the 7D page, and the 50th year. I am in my Mars period. We can see two cards of influence for that period: the 10H and the 5C. We will use the 10H for now.

Here's the secret: look at the whole hand of the 10H.

Now I have a card for each category of my life during this period.

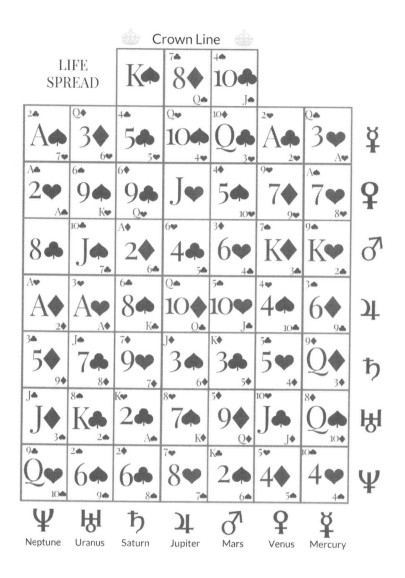

LIFE SPREAD

Crown Line

12

SAMPLE READING FROM PAULA'S LIFE: USING THE WHOLE HAND

Find the 10H in the chart above. Its Moon card is to the right. (4S) All other cards in its hand stretch out to the left, and then down. Let's take the whole hand of the 10H and ask these planetary questions:

Moon: What will I be feeling? What is my emotional task? 4S is the answer. (Moon card for the 10H) I will be finding or creating my own sense of security through my home. This is true. I am clearing out old stuff, making it nicer, and we are just beginning our search for a new home. Big theme of home!

This gives me amazing fulfillment. (a 4 thing)

Mercury: What will I be thinking about during this period? What will my mental activity center around?

10D is my Mercury card now. (1 to the left the 10H...are you catching on?) I will be thinking about a large sum of money and be pulled in every direction.

With the QC as karma to the 10D, there will also be themes of teaching. This is so. We have just launched www.itiskismet.com at the time of this writing, and I am focused on teaching through this book as well as adjusting my mind to making more money.

Also, my mind has a definite Jupitarian energy right now: very expansive and positive.

(Notice everything: The 10D is at the Jupiter/Jupiter intersection. This simple intersection will tell you a LOT!)

Venus: What will I be enjoying? What will my relationships feel like? What are the themes around home, or women?

8S is my Venus card. Power, strength, will, possibly control and discipline. I have been much more disciplined with my private yoga practice and my diet. I am also surrounded by powerful women!

[Do you see? You can use this method for any single card of influence, whether it is a yearly card, or a 13 year card!]

Mars: What will I be passionate and pragmatic about, taking action, feeling angry about, or even what will turn me on?

Ace H is the answer. I will be highly motivated about new beginnings, birth, and all the 'babies' in my life. This also represents my inner child. And indeed, we are birthing Kismet, and I am birthing this book! Also, I have been more pragmatic in taking care of my inner child: good diet, good bed time, good yoga, chocolate, movies, and kindness!

Jupiter: Where will I be successful, what is the source of my blessing, and how will I be challenged to expand?

AD is Jupiter to me now. All Aces represent desire for something. Diamonds represent money. So the desire for money will be an asset to me. It's a great time to focus on my financial desires, to envision wealth. It's a great time to do manifesting work!

Also, Aces are beginnings. I am being challenged to expand into this. Jupiter is like the Universe saying, "I dare you to find out how successful you can be with this! For you surely will be."

I can't tell you how accurate this is. My Guides have been telling me, "Write a list of what you want! Do your manifesting juju!!!" I know this practice is in the flow because it's easy. That's how Jupiter feels.

[This is a good time to point out that we each have our unique relationships to every planet. Jupiter is not natural to me. It feels like my beloved father, AD, who a Sagittarius, and a bit reckless at times. He loved risk and adventure. I'm not so crazy about it.

I am actually more comfortable with Saturn, even if it is challenging! No wonder; Mom is a Capricorn! LOL!]

Dad and Mom

Saturn: What will be difficult, challenging, and a pain in my rear? What has karma, or a sense of destiny and timing during this period?

QD is my pain in the rear. The Diamond women in my life have been speaking the truth to me and not so gently at times!

15

Also, I have been spiritually connected through my writing. [The cards can validate your strengths as much as show you where you need to grow.]

Pluto: What will trigger me in a big way? What needs to die so something can be reborn?

3S is my transformation card now. This is the card of internal beauty being manifested in the physical world. (The Artist's card) Bringing my soul into form will be my biggest challenge during this time. "Making it real" with the website and this book hold the key to that transformation. Spot on. The 3S also indicates being pulled between 2 different things. The website and this book would certainly fit!

That's all for the 10H. I could do the same for the 5C. And yes, they are connected...

Each card in the hand of the 5C would augment the corresponding card in the 10H hand.

Let's dial the lens of time back a bit, and adjust the focus to see that this period has, indeed, been focused on Mars. Mars is career, action, the body, and pragmatism. Every aspect of my life this period has been focused on those things. And one period leads into the next...

All of the details I have been chasing will come together as a whole for my Jupiter period. Mars says, "What actions are you taking?" Jupiter will ask me, "What is the bigger picture? What is the enterprise? Let's see some success!"

Dial the lens back further, and we see age 50 is the 2nd of a 7 yr. period, being ruled by Venus. When I ask, "What aspect of Venus has been in focus for me?", I see that it is the quality of beauty. I have been obsessed with the color and 'aesthetic' of my daily life.

YOUR READING

Go to your page in COD, find your cards of influence for this 52 day period, and begin with the top card, as your 'sun' card. Then write out the hand of that card, using the Life Spread on page 12.

Moon*
Sun
Mercury
Venus
Mars
Jupiter
Saturn
Uranus
Neptune
Pluto

Remember, the Moon card is to the right of the card. For example, if your top card of influence (Sun card) is the 7C, the moon card would be the 9H.

Then proceeding to the left and down from the card, write in the next 8 cards of the hand, in the order of the planets listed on the page above. For the 7C example, the Mercury card would be the 5D, Venus: QS, Mars: JC, etc.

Fill them in and then find each card in the following list for the interpretation.

PLANETARY MEANINGS

As a reminder, these are the issues, events, and "questions" that each planetary position is presenting:

MOON: How will I be feeling? What will give me a sense of comfort and safety? Mother events and issues.

MERCURY: What or who will I be thinking about? How will my mind be operating? Short trips, ideas, my car.

VENUS: What will give me pleasure and fun? Issues around home, relationship, and the feminine in my life.

MARS: What will I be taking action for? What will I be feeling passionate, angry, or pragmatic about? Issues with body, sex, physical activity, career, and the masculine in my life.

JUPITER: What will bring me blessings, financial and otherwise? How will I be challenged to expand and actualize my potential? Issues with entrepreneurial business, father figures, success.

SATURN: Where will I be challenged to make corrections? How will I be challenged to grow? What are my karmic appointments at this time? Issues connected to father figures, health, and destiny.

URANUS: Where will my brilliance shine? How will I demonstrate my natural genius? Who or what will be unpredictable or unreliable? Issues with real estate (where you live), expansion of consciousness, humanitarian things.

NEPTUNE: What will I be dreaming about? Who or what will I idealize and not see clearly? Who will I project my stuff onto? Issues around spirituality, dreams, addictions

PLUTO: What has to die so something can be reborn? Who or what will be deeply triggering? What needs transformation or what will be the source of my transformation? Issues around release, death, power.

PAULA'S CARD INTERPRETATIONS

Keep in mind that any of these cards can be the birth card of someone in your life. It could also be their karma card, their planetary ruler, or a card in their hand, which will show you the specific aspect of that person relevant to you at the time. Is it a card in your hand? If it is your Saturn card, for example, that particular life challenge is up for you.

SPADES

Physical realm, inclusive of all suits: emotional, mental, financial or values, and pragmatic

KS Assured success in overcoming obstacles, issues of responsibility (are you taking too much or too little?) and the job of defining your own reality. Circle of 7 person. Spade male.

QS Big picture perspective, role as coach or mentor, realizing that you are solely responsible for your circumstances, life, and fulfillment. "It's up to me." Spade female

JS Spiritual initiation: your life is being turned inside out, upside down, and you have to navigate differently. Is there deception or theft in your midst? Is it time to be a magician? Young Spade person.

10S Your plate is very, very full. Success with hard work is assured. Possible addiction issues. Make sure you take some time for rest and self-care. Redefine success for yourself.

9S Completion on physical plane. Death of something. Harvest, ending, reaching for a larger context to understand your life.

8S Physical strength, discipline, power. Stubbornness, being an advocate for the truth, own your perspective.

7S Feels like you are walking through oatmeal. You will be very sensitive to anything that is out of alignment with the truth. Great time for a spiritual practice, especially in Uranus or Neptune, like mantra and meditation. Possible health issues, obstacles, integrity. Look at the physical aspects of your life that may need adjusting, such as diet or sleep. YOU WILL GET THROUGH THIS!!

6S "What is my purpose? What is the plan?" Your hunger to know is designed so that you pay attention. Information is coming. Be assured. Smoothing of affairs, balance, big picture perspectives.

5S Strongest indication for a move when it's in Venus or Uranus. Change, trip, relocation. Change in how you navigate. Importance of PRESENCE. Be like a child, scientist, or traveler. Have fun! This may be a time for adventure!

4S Security is hi-lighted. Any feelings of insecurity will come to the surface where your security depends on outside circumstances. This works like homeopathic medicine. The result will be security if your affirmation is "I make myself safe." Issues around house or home may be up.

3S Involvements in 2 different locations, feeling pulled in 2 directions. This is not necessarily about choosing yet. Artist card: are you actuating your deep soul expression into the physical?

2S Friendship, companionship, someone with whom you do stuff. This is also a call to become your own best friend. Are you on board with yourself? Your heart, your mind your desires?

AS Transformation, rebirth. A new beginning in the physical realm, a new career. Secrets, esoteric knowledge, this card system, a new forging of your identity, aloneness, defining yourself. See also 7H. (self) betrayal or forgiveness?

DIAMONDS

Values and desires, money. What is important, worthwhile.

KD Being the King in your Kingdom of values. You will have a strong sense of integrity and a graciousness of spirit. Success in the business realm, especially if you own your business.

QD Service oriented business, successful business woman. What are your values in terms of service? Also, her role is to speak the truth where it may hurt. A Diamond female or you yourself may be filling this role.

JD Your own business. Young entrepreneur, young Diamond male, possible manipulation thru charm; sales. Card of the U.S.A. Great sense of humor, creativity, ingenuity. See also JC.

10D Big chunk of $$, great financial success. But just as likely $ will come and go thru your hands. You may be pulled in every direction, be the center of activity, networker, or a Switchboard operator. Visualize being a tree, taking in the sun of Source, branching out, blossoming!

9D Financial generosity or loss. Money going out. Need for surrender. Feelings of poverty or a lack of value. Intuition, care-taking, peace maker. Nonprofit, fundraiser. Being of service (too much or too little?)

8D Conviction around your values: clarity about what you will no longer settle for, what you must insist on. Stubbornness, being a jerk, or a noble advocate for the truth. Financial power.

7D Self-doubt, self-esteem issues. The Universe is using its fine-toothed comb to examine the foundation of your self-worth. Short-cut: "I am worthy because I exist. I have a unique gift to give. I love myself." This may also indicate a C-7 person. See also the 9H.

6D Destined work, karmic balance around money, being paid what is owed or paying what you owe. Clarity around purpose, receiving messages around "the plan." Contracts.

5D A change in what you value, in how income arrives, or traveling for business. Freedom, independence, fun!

4D Financial stability, having just enough, or a call to gain clarity about desires. 10% of people experience this as hard work for gain. The other 90% will experience this as the 5S: moving, traveling, major change, or to be PRESENT and enjoy your 5 senses.

3D Two jobs, being pulled between 2 desires. It may not be time to decide yet. Sit with it. Possible worry or creativity re. money. The need to express your values.

2D Partnership in desire or values, business partnership. The deeper meaning is to get on board with your own desires and values; be your own business partner.

AD New beginning in desire or money, new job. Learning to value yourself. Time alone, define your desires. Great manifesting energy! Make a list of your desires and feel their fulfillment.

CLUBS

Concepts, ideas, teaching, writing, speaking. Consciousness, beliefs, philosophy.

KC Mastery of mind/beliefs. Owning your truth. Sovereignty of one's perspective. Success with mind-related things: education, learning, teaching. Man of the Club suit, man of knowledge. Possible arrogance.

QC Wisdom, intuition, psychic ability. Coach or teacher, woman of Club suit, of wisdom. Possible impatience, irritability, due to being able to anticipate more intuitively than others.

JC Brilliant, original ideas. One who is charming, impulsive, immature, manipulative, great lover, fantastic sense of humor. This person could be you at this time. Young man of the Club suit or man who is in his 'Jack.'

10C Success with mentally related endeavors. Intense focus on career. Big perspective, strength and independence. Jerk tendencies. Be a nice jerk! Lots of Mars energy: passion, energy, action.

9C Open mindedness, allowing all perspectives. Ending of old belief system, idea, or involvement with education. Let go of that old, limiting paradigm! Mediator, counselor.

8C Powerful, possibly fixed mind. (That means really stubborn!) Information from past lives coming through. Circle of 7 person.

7C Discernment, analysis, insight. Tendency to judge, especially the self. Quit that! Discern but be kind. You may be dealing with a betrayal of trust and the need to forgive. Don't forgive too soon. This is a time for understanding and owning your internal landscape. Nobody is out to get you.

6C Balanced perspective, compromise, common sense, mediator. Also you will wonder what the plan or karmic contracts are at this time. That's good, because this card indicates that information is coming.

5C Change of mind, restlessness and dissatisfaction. Need for change. Take note of what you do not want right now, translate those things into what you DO want. This is a time of clarification. Also fun and social engagement!

4C Are you getting clear about what you think? Your clearly defined ideas can give you a sense of security, but don't become rigid about them either. This card also indicates dealing with packages of information, from organizing your files to writing a paper.

3C You may be doing some writing during this time, or expanding your concepts. You may also be pulled between two concepts or ideas. This is a creative energy so you will need to express yourself somehow or it may turn into worry.

2C Conversations, (in Mars it can be aggressive), sharing ideas. This is often a card of fears, or your internal conversation. Use this time to introduce more kindness to your dealings with yourself and your mind. Navel gazing.

AC New beginning in the realm of ideas, new mental project, or a desire for information. Self-focus. Try to avoid narcissism! Alone time, loneliness. Circle of 7 person. See also the 2H.

HEARTS

Love, emotional realm, relationships.

KH Graciousness, ability to hold large emotional container for a group. Fatherhood, an emotionally mature man, pragmatic, kind management of people. Man of the Heart suit. Potential for anxiety. Nurture inner child.

QH Mother, wife, lover issues. Bliss. Sex, especially in Mars. Bipolarity between pleasure and work-a-holism. Possible addiction issues. Bliss can be sought through addiction, sex, and/or union with the Divine. Woman of the Heart suit.

JH Children, initiation into loving better, perhaps through sacrifice of some kind. Young man of Heart suit. Great time for deepening one's spiritual connection, especially when it is in Uranus or Neptune.

10H Happiness with a group of people, being visible to the public, leading or teaching a group. You may feel extroverted and inspired, but you may also need to balance group activity with alone time. Busy, busy time.

9H Need for unconditional love. Loss or ending of a relationship. Grief work. This is a tough one, I know. Rebirth of a relationship. This card can also indicate taking on the role of a counselor, feelings of unconditional love, or a focus on one's self worth. See also the 7D.

8H Emotional charm, power, charisma, healing energy.
This emotional power can be used to attract people, manage or try to control them, or even heal them. I call it the "grow some balls card," for those who need some encouragement to claim their power!

7H Emotional attachment. You will feel anything that is out of alignment with love; therefore you may seem especially sensitive. Also indicated: disappointment (let go of those expectations), and forgiveness. This can be a tough card. Not gonna lie to ya!

6H Karmic or destined relationship, or balancing of emotional realm. Hungry to know your purpose? Or find your soul mate? Information is coming, so pay attention. Does a relationship need balancing? Karmic repayment?

5H Feelings of restlessness, dissatisfaction. Easier for odd #'d cards, very difficult for even carded people. It's time to reassess what you want, what or who feels good in your life. What's more important than a big change is the clarity that will come from identifying both what you want and what you do not want. Don't hid from that! This is also a great card for enjoying people. I call it the "bartender's card." You may be very socially magnetic at this time.

4H What makes you feel emotionally secure and safe? What gives you comfort? This will be on the front burner now, and you will probably start out feeling insecure. That's the homeopathic medicine working! Your job now is to make yourself feel safe.

3H Indecision, date around, don't make a commitment. You may feel pulled between two things or people you love, or there may be 3 important people in your midst. (may or may not include you.) Love 'outside the box' time.

2H Intimate relationship. This may be with a baby, your beloved, yourself, or the Divine. This card indicates beautiful loving connectedness. 2's are always a call to cultivate a deeper relationship to the self. Become your own beloved. Circle of 7 person. See also the AC.

AH Birth of something beloved: you, a baby, a relationship. This is THE card of creation, so get out your manifesting tools and imagine the life you want. This is also a seed energy for love. Yearning is the seed. Be clear about what or who you are calling in. Focus on inner child.

SEEING PATTERNS: WHEN AND HOW DO LR CARDS SHOW UP?

Now let's go back to your page in the COD. When you look over the present year you are in (your age), are there any cards that repeat during the year? This is often the case.

When I first do a reading for someone, I look for themes. One card may appear both in your Venus period, and as your long range card. This is a clue as to when that influence will be the most active. It may also indicate the area of your life that it will most affect. For example, having the 5S as a LR card means a big change. If the 5S also appears in your Venus period, it may happen at that time, or it means that you will move, since Venus affects home. If the 5S appeared in your Mercury period, it may mean you are just thinking about a big change or trip this year.

A more subtle level of investigation is possible here. An all year card (LR, Pluto/Result, etc) may appear in the hand of your card of influence for any given period. In the sample reading for myself, (year 50 for the 7D), we saw that I have the 3C in Neptune for my Mars period. (because 3C is the Neptune card for the 10H) Then as I look at my whole year, I see that the 3C is also my Pluto card. What this means is that I will experience a kind of transformation through my writing, especially during my Mars period. Mars indicates that the writing is career related. As Neptune to the 10H, it means that my writing will be a spiritual connection for me. And indeed, that has all been true.

If I want to pursue the writing theme, I can look for the 3C in the hands of any of my planetary period cards.

This is to help calm your mind in case I scrambled it.

SUITS AND NUMBERS

Another way themes show up is with a predominance of the same suit or number. Lots of Hearts mean that your emotional development will be a priority. Lots of Diamonds mean finances and desires are at the forefront. Clubs- concepts and learning, Spades-lifestyle, the practical. Many 5's will indicate lots of change--all kinds of change. You may take all year to make necessary adjustments. See if any obvious themes pop up, especially when you are thinking about a particular issue.

You may be surprised at how obvious it is, and how validating it can be to find your life in a few printed symbols! I have burst out sobbing more than once to see that my grief or joy or struggle or even ease had a sense of timing and purpose.

"To everything there is a season, and a time for every purpose under heaven." Ecclesiates 3:1

TIPS FOR USING YOUR INTUITION

I have often told clients that this is mostly a matter of learning to trust yourself. We receive information in a variety of ways constantly. We have just been trained to ignore everything except our mind and our physical needs. A divinatory tool is a wonderful way to nurture and experiment with intuition.

In the context of the cards, I think of the little girl, Lyra, in the Golden Compass series by Philip Pullman. In it, she finds an "Alethiometer," which means "truth meter." It's like a clock with symbols around the outside instead of numbers.

When she forms a question in her mind, she gazes at the dials, which point to a few symbols. There are a variety of meanings to each symbol. (Sound familiar yet?) She describes taking her mind down a kind of elevator with each symbol. She feels for the pause in the elevator when it reaches a level where the specific meaning is indicated.

Learn to feel into that subtle urge, no matter how strange it may seem. My Guides have referenced a card for a particular meaning which I had never encountered before. It's a great way to deepen your understanding of the cards. This process can become very esoteric!

I can scarcely explain it better than this. Put your hand on your heart or your belly and listen. Close your eyes and see.
With this card system, I have learned that multiple meanings will apply for one card. For example, with the 3S, you can be pulled between two different locations, and you can also be focused on your artistic side. The QH will bring sex, but she will also bring mother issues and a tendency to dive into your favorite addiction.

You will know pretty quickly what is going on for you, if you stay in the present and tune into your subtle bodies. (emotional, mental, spiritual).

If you want to go into the future, just know that the further you go, the cloudier it will become. There are certain destined events that you may feel into, but there is so much free will and so many variables, that many expressions of any card are possible. My advice is to stay with the present, the most recent period, and the upcoming one if it is less than 3 weeks away. Most importantly, leave fear out of the equation. Nothing gums up the works like fear, with its close cousin, attachment. If you are surrendered to the wisdom and love of your Higher Power (whatever that may be), clarity comes more easily.

Try not to ask Yes/No questions. If at all possible, an open ended question like "Tell me about..." will allow the Universe to paint with color instead of black and white. And yes, do pray or meditate, and ask for clear guidance before you start. Your Guides LOVE to communicate with you. But remember, there are things they will not discuss with you, for your own good.

I hope this has been helpful. Feel free to drop me a line or ask a question, at littleinkeeper@gmail.com (yes, there is only one 'n').

Schedule a reading through our fabulous website, kismet.cards or my personal website, paulajkrueger.com.

You can also get on our (Kismet's) email list to learn about upcoming classes and events by signing up for your FREE Pluto report after you enter your birthday.

Much Love,

Paula

39922201R00021